SCHOLASTIC SCIENCE READERS™

LEVEL
1
AGES 5 AND 6

TORNADOES

BRIAN CASSIE

SCHOLASTIC
REFERENCE

PHOTO CREDITS: Cover: Corbis. Page 1, 3: Corbis; 4: Richard Bart Green/*Deseret News*/Liaison Agency by Getty Images; 5: Charlie Riedel/Liaison Agency by Getty Images; 6, 7: SuperStock; 9: Jim Zuckerman/Corbis; 10: *Miami Herald*/Liaison Agency by Getty Images; 11: C. C. Lockwood/Bruce Coleman Inc.; 13: SuperStock; 14–15: Michael S. Yamashita/Corbis; 16: Howard B. Bluestein/Photo Researchers, Inc.; 17: Corbis; 18: Howard Bluestein/Photo Researchers, Inc.; 19: Jim Mone/AP Wide World Photos; 20: Warren Faidley/Weatherstock; 21: Curtis Compton/*Atlanta Journal Constitution*/AP Wide World Photos; 22: Corbis Sygma; 23: Charlie Riedel/Liaison Agency by Getty Images; 24: Warren Faidley/Weatherstock; 27: Kent F. Berg/*The Herald*/Liaison Agency by Getty Images; 28: Howard Bluestein/Photo Researchers, Inc.; 29: Neil Jacobs/Liaison Agency by Getty Images; 30: Corbis.

ISBN 0-439-26990-3

Book design by Barbara Balch and Kay Petronio
Photo research by Sarah Longacre

20 19 18 17 16   05 06

Printed in the U.S.A. 23

First printing, May 2002

We are grateful to Francie Alexander, reading specialist, and
to Adele M. Brodkin, Ph.D., developmental psychologist,
for their contributions to the development of this series.

Our thanks also to our science consultant Jonathan D. W. Kahl,
Professor of Atmospheric Sciences, University of Wisconsin-Milwaukee.

Tornadoes are very wild and dangerous storms. These storms do not happen often. When tornadoes *do* happen, people sometimes call them **twisters**.

A tornado is a spinning
storm with very, very strong
winds. The winds spin in a
circle.

A tornado is shaped like a **funnel** or a cone. The tornado reaches from the clouds all the way to the ground.

Some tornadoes are fat.
Some tornadoes are skinny.
But all tornadoes are powerful.

Tornadoes form when warm,
wet air meets cool, dry air high
up in the sky.

The warm air and the cool air have lots of energy. If the two types of air push each other hard enough, this can make a thunderstorm.

Thunderstorms are huge clouds with lightning and thunder. They also have strong winds.

Tornadoes sometimes form in the middle of big, powerful thunderstorms. The air in the storm spins around very fast. It moves two ways. The air spins around in a circle. The air also moves up very fast in the middle of the circle.

Sometimes, the spinning winds drop down out of the clouds and reach the ground. When this happens, we call the storm a tornado.

A tornado that forms over water is called a **waterspout**. Waterspouts can be very fat or very skinny, just like tornadoes that form over land.

You may have seen pictures of tornadoes. But not many people will ever see a real tornado.

Have you ever wondered what it is like to see a tornado in person?

Before a tornado, the sky gets dark. Sometimes, the clouds turn green.

Next, the wind starts to blow. Pretty soon it is really blowing.

With the wind comes rain. It can rain very, very hard when a tornado is coming.

With the wind and the rain come thunder and lightning.

The wind gets even stronger. With the strong wind and bright lightning and booming thunder comes **hail**. Hail is balls of ice that form inside thunderstorms. Usually, hail is small, but it can sometimes be as big as baseballs.

Then, with all of the wind and rain and thunder and lightning and hail comes the tornado itself.

The winds in a tornado
are the fastest on Earth. They
move much faster than the
fastest race cars. They make
an awesome noise as they
spin around.

Up close, a tornado sounds
like 100 trains all zooming by
at once. People who hear a
tornado never forget the sound.

Tornadoes are so powerful that they can pick up things and throw them in the air. Tornadoes can blow small buildings down.

In places where tornadoes are common, people have special tornado shelters under the ground.

If there is no special tornado
shelter, the basement is the
best place to be. Never stay
near a window, since the glass
almost always breaks and flies
around during a tornado.

Scientists who study tornadoes have invented weather machines that tell them where tornadoes might form. The scientists call for a **tornado watch** if the weather looks like a tornado might happen.

If a tornado is actually spotted, a **tornado warning** is given on television and radio. People must pay attention to these warnings. They need to seek shelter right away if there is a tornado spotted in their area.

Where are tornadoes common? The United States has the most tornadoes in the world.

The middle part of the United States and the state of Florida have the most tornadoes.

The center of the United States, from Texas up into Nebraska and Iowa, has the biggest tornadoes. This area is called **Tornado Alley.**

People who live in this part of the United States know what to do if a tornado comes.

A tornado near Pampa, Texas

Florida has the most tornadoes, but not the biggest ones. Florida also has the most waterspouts.

Tornadoes and waterspouts happen over much of the earth. Most of them form in spring and summer.

Tornadoes usually form
late in the afternoon.

Tornadoes are truly wonders of nature.

Glossary

funnel—a shape like a cone

hail—round chunks of ice that form in thunderstorms

Tornado Alley—part of the center of the United States that gets many big tornadoes every year

tornado warning—an announcement that a tornado has been spotted

tornado watch—a warning that a tornado might form

tornadoes—very powerful, spinning storms

twisters—another name for tornadoes

waterspout—a tornado that forms over water

A Note to Parents

L earning to read is such an exciting time in a child's life. You may delight in sharing your favorite fairy tales and picture books with your child.

But don't forget the importance of introducing your child to the world of nonfiction. The ability to read and comprehend factual material will be essential to your child in school and throughout life. The Scholastic Science Readers™ series was created especially with beginning readers in mind. These books, with their clear texts and beautiful photographs, will help you to share the wonders of science with *your* new reader.

Suggested Activity

Y ou have just learned that tornadoes are powerful storms. Scientists who study tornadoes must be very careful not to get caught in a tornado's path.

Here's something simple you can do to learn more about staying safe in a tornado. Ask an adult to help you go to the website for the National Severe Storm Laboratory. This is a laboratory where scientists study all types of storms, including tornadoes. The website has a coloring book you can print out. The coloring book has three parts and is called "*Billy and Maria Learn About Tornado Safety.*" While you are coloring in the pictures, you'll be getting tips about how you and your family can stay safe if a tornado comes!

Go to this web address, and click on the picture of Billy and Maria: **http://www.nssl.noaa.gov/edu/bm**